UN MOMENTO

A Taste of
Italian-American Pastimes

GINA FAVA

ALSO BY GINA FAVA

NOVELS

The H.E.L.L. Ranger Series

The Race.

Formula

Stand-Alone Suspense Thriller

The Sculptor

UN MOMENTO

A Taste of
Italian-American Pastimes

GINA FAVA

Steepo Press

℗

New York, Boston

To my family, then and now. Vi voglio bene assai.

COPYRIGHT

2018 Gina Fava

PUBLISHING HISTORY:

Steepo Press, Paperback and Digital Copy

Cover Design and Photographer: Gina Fava

Print ISBN: 978-0-9893587-8-1

Ebook ISBN: 978-0-9893587-4-3

CONTENTS

INTRODUCTION

Isn't it funny how old-fashioned notions make their way into the present? Decades ago my grandparents would return from visits to Italy with sweet, decadent jars of hazelnut cocoa spread. Now it's an American kitchen staple known as Nutella. The woolen pullover my great-grandmother knit for my dad is now my teenage daughter's ski sweater. And bocce courts, once prevalent only among seniors in tight-knit Italian communities, are now popping up across the country in backyards and behind taverns.

This book is a collection of short essays about my Italian-American life, each one a personal reflection on old-fashioned notions that have found their way into today. The essays represent an authentic nostalgic journey toward new trends, and they draw from my regular column in *Bostoniano* magazine, as well as work published in *Buffalo Magazine, Bucket List Publications*, and *StudyBridgeInternational.com*. Whatever your own cultural heritage, you might find that you can relate to many or all of them. I've also included never-before-published, traditional family recipes that are oft-requested and crazy delicious. Unfortunately, you won't find my sauce or meatball recipes. I've been sworn to secrecy, and they remain highly classified information. However, as a bonus, and to allay any hurt feelings for my non-disclosure, I've asked my sommelier husband, Jamie, to pair every dish with THE perfect wine for your dining pleasure. In the end, my hope is that my stories and these recipes will inspire you to learn, share, and experience more about Italian culture and that of your own.

As an author, I typically write novels featuring Americans knee-deep in Italian intrigue, and my readers often ask me about my Italian background. I'm a native of Buffalo, New York, residing with my husband and children in New

England. My grandparents and father immigrated to Buffalo from Tuscany when he was a boy, over fifty years ago. There, he met my Italian-American mother, and together they raised me and my two younger brothers. I graduated from the University at Buffalo and later earned a law degree, but it was the bomb scares and car chases I endured while studying international business at the American University of Rome that spurred my interest in writing suspense novels. It's also where I met my husband, Jamie, an Italian-American from Boston. Together, we share children, wine stores, and dogs who obey commands in Italian.

On "Pasta Sundays," my family cranks up the Bocelli and we roll out homemade pasta for friends, family, and anyone else we can convince to try my sauce. Our dozen or so backyard vines will likely never produce enough crop to yield even a bottle, which is why we own wine stores—because homemade pasta and wine always go hand in hand. Now and again we return to Italy, where we gather research for my writing, visit wineries, and reconnect with our Tuscan relatives.

The title of this book, *Un Momento,* is a phrase I grew up with, my dad's response anytime my mom called him for dinner, and one I still hear today from my son whenever I'm calling him for dinner. What's past is present again. What we gaze upon as a treasured memory often reinvents itself into a life lesson. Italian culture imbues everyday life with flavor, like a hearty dish of ravioli on Pasta Sunday. Take a moment to linger over stories of tradition, family, food, wine, art, travel, and other morsels rich with Italian heritage. You might stumble upon a few that invoke a bit of nostalgia, or that perhaps incite a desire to learn, share, and experience more about the Italian culture or that of your own.

HERITAGE

WICKED GOOD ITALIAN DIALECTS

A visit to my father's hometown of Abbadia San Salvatore in Siena gave me interesting insight into the concept of dialect. Our relatives had taken us to a local restaurant, and the cousins who'd moved out of town ordered *una lattina di Coca-Cola*, or a can of Coke. Those relatives who still resided in town similarly ordered Cokes, but pronounced it much differently, dropping the hard *c* sound entirely, instead asking for "Ola-Ola." Similarly, a native Bostonian typically drops a letter (like an *r*.) Both instances give language a flair all its own, and certainly give the listener an indication of heritage.

As a native of Buffalo, where the words *berry*, *Barry*, and *bury* are pronounced the same way, where *pop* means *soda* and the words *hot* and *cod* take on a nasally, back-of-the-throat twang, it's clear to me that my husband, Jamie, who hails from north of Boston, speaks differently. When he says the word *pattern*, I must rely on context to determine whether he's saying *Patton*, *pattin'*, or *patent*. When I first met my husband's mom on Cape Cod, she suggested, "Relax, go put ya shahts on." I merely stared back at her, confounded. Jamie translated, "Gina, my mom's asking you to change from wearing pants and into shorts." I smiled and nodded, and she and I have gotten along swimmingly since then. The same is likely true for many New Englanders and their extended families. Their backgrounds—whether they hail from the city of Boston or surrounding regions—determine their particular pronunciation, grammar, or vocabulary. But like my mom's minestrone, it's variety that makes life flavorful.

The factors that typically influence the development of dialects in a region or country include geographical location (people living in close proximity to each other, as well as people living in isolation from others); socioeconomic conditions; complex colonial history; movement of ancestors; strong regional loyalties; and the cultural influence of nearby communities. In such regions or countries, a dialect that is commonly used in the media (as in entertainment and news programming) may be very different from the dialect used in official government business, in schools' curricula, and in everyday street language. For example, a Boston news anchor may articulate the English language differently than a meter reader in Quincy. Either way, they both get their points across, one perhaps more colorfully than the other.

There are two major groups of Italian dialects—northern and southern, divided by the Spezia-Rimini regional line running across Italy from west to east. The northern groups are either based in Veneto and speak a Venetic dialect, or of the Gallo-Italic group that encompasses most of the rest of the region and is influenced by Celtic speech. As for the southern part of the boot, the most common Italian dialects include:

- Tuscan (most of Tuscany);
- Abruzzese, Pugliese, Umbrian (near Tuscany);
- Laziale, Central Marchigiano (in and around Rome);
- Those common to the southern part of Italy (like Napolitano); and
- Those indicative of the outermost regions of the south, including Calabrese, Apulian, and Sardinian dialects.

The rich variety speaks to the turmoil that Italy endured on the way to its unification in 1861. In Italy, only an official republic since 1946, cultural pride is highly regional to this day. Though the Tuscan dialect is considered the national language or the *lingua italiana*, perhaps because the area is considered the birthplace of Italian literature (as in Dante, Petrarca, and Boccaccio), the different regions still proudly embrace the differences that distinguish their manner of speaking from others in their country, much like Bostonians, or Southerners, or Midwesterners.

There are many other countries with multiple dialects of the same language, including Spain (ten dialects), India (about two thousand dialects), Asia (Japan has dozens, and China has over two hundred dialects), and many more. Dialects add color to language and infuse flavor into culture. After all, wouldn't one rather have "wicked good" cannoli than just good cannoli?

LA PASSEGGIATA

Italians value *la passeggiata*, which is not just a walk about town for fresh air or physical exercise but also a chance to connect with local community on a daily basis. A centuries-old tradition in small towns across Italy, the passeggiata typically involves Italians donning fashionable attire, dispensing with cell phones, and actively socializing face-to-face with family and friends, ambling through the main streets of town and culminating in the central piazza. The custom typically takes place in the evening, when school and work have finished and Italians are winding down before a small evening meal. The passeggiata is a lovely opportunity to reconnect with neighbors.

Children play, adolescents flirt, neighbors gossip, and old friends meet new ones. Strolling through the streets hand in hand or arm in arm signifies camaraderie among all people, young and old, of any gender. It's a time to window-shop, walk the dog, stop for a spritzer, grab a gelato, or catch up for a few minutes on a park bench. As the sun sets and stars begin to dot the sky, it's a great opportunity to relish a bit of leisure.

Whenever my family travels to Italy, the passeggiata pastime is special. It's something I first noticed as a child in my dad's hometown of Abbadia San Salvatore in Siena. Aunts, uncles, and cousins of our extended family would head out nearly every night, sometimes beneath umbrellas or wrapped in heavy coats or sporting new sandals, depending on the time of year. They'd hug and kiss cheeks with each other and with their neighbors as if it had been a long spell since their last passeggiata, which had actually been only the night before. Maybe the hospitable custom of the passeggiata is the reason Italian families and friends remain so loyal and close. It fosters the enduring concept of *la famiglia.*

The tradition has indeed made its way across the ocean. Growing up, I loved when my Italian neighbors in Buffalo would congregate on their front porches in the early evening and share the day's events. In the North End of Boston, Italians uphold similar means of socializing, whether in the afternoon while walking home from school or work, or in the evening on the way to a local restaurant. The cobblestone streets, the corner-store Italian ice, and the aroma of espresso likely lend to the Italian experience. Other cities embrace strolling among Little Italy districts, such as the historic Federal Hill in Providence and the famous Little Italy in Manhattan. Still others have developed walkways expressly for communing with others and nature, like the Harborwalk in Boston, Canalside in Buffalo, the Cliffwalk in Newport, the Boardwalk in New Jersey, or even the Las Vegas strip. Not all passeggiate are expressly Italian in feel, but the concept of connecting with community remains the same.

Passeggiata is a part of Italian culture that I've tried to incorporate into my everyday life. If I'm on vacation, the best way to get to know a new town is to take a stroll after twilight. Likewise, after a long day of work or play, I love clearing up the dinner dishes and heading outside for a walk. It's a chance to reconnect with my family and neighbors, and to appreciate the wildlife dwelling in my yard, like the family of woodchucks that reside beneath the tool shed or the wild turkey loitering in the woods.

There are many reasons one chooses to participate in passeggiata, whether to catch up with others, to get in touch with nature, to meet someone new, or to lose oneself in one's own thoughts. All it takes is some comfortable shoes and an open heart.

FOOD FOR THOUGHT:
LEARNING TO SPEAK ITALIAN

My dad came to America over half a century ago and spoke only Italian, but now he speaks English like a native-born American and sometimes finds himself at a loss for some Italian words. Similarly, my husband and I spent a lot of time learning Italian in school, only to watch it evaporate over the course of time. Do you wish you were fluent in Italian? Or perhaps you've lost a lot of language skill for lack of usage? Or maybe your family is looking for a crash course on the basics for an upcoming trip to Italy? Whatever the reason one may wish to augment or maintain the ability to converse in Italian, there's an array of methods that will fit any lifestyle. Whether it's five minutes a day or five hours, there are many ways to increase vocabulary or to tweak grammar and pronunciation.

For those who appreciate face-to-face, traditional learning, there are helpful interactive Italian language classes with a teacher scheduled in most major cities. They range in price and learning levels, and they differ based on adult/children lessons, private or small group sizes, and possible inclusion of cultural education such as cooking, fashion, and literature. Whether you drop in after work to avoid the commuter crunch or pack up the kids for a Saturday-morning trip to the city, there are many flexible options, which may include:

- Dante Alighieri Society
- Berlitz Learning Center
- The Language Institute
- A local community college or center for Adult Education

If you're on the go and don't have time for a traditional classroom setting, there's a diverse assortment of Italian language software and applications for your PC and smartphone to accommodate quick bites of virtual learning. Some are simple translation apps, for basic conversation in a travel situation. Simply speak or type English sentences into these apps and instantly retrieve the Italian translation to order food or to buy a museum ticket. Other software applications provide more in-depth learning. These include exercises for translation, themed vocabulary units, dialogue repetition, and flashcards. Some offer proficiency tracking systems, challenge-building games and quizzes, and progress reports. Others are aimed at people looking to practice with matched linguists, allowing for live or text conversations in a safe, friendly online environment. Some are free or low-cost apps, and others are more expensive, yet comprehensive software programs. Here are just a few of the many applications available:

- iTranslate
- Google Translate
- Duolingo
- Memrise
- Babbel
- LingQ
- HelloTalk
- Rosetta Stone
- Berlitz

I've tried nearly all of them, and some work better for me than others. My favorite is the Duolingo application on my phone. It provides quick lessons while I'm standing in a bank line or waiting at my son's hockey practice. I've vastly improved my grammar and vocabulary in less than a year by competing with my own personal score or else competing against Jamie. We encourage each other to strive for more and share what we've learned in conversation.

Of course, whatever your level of fluency, there's programming available as entertainment, as more or less "cultural comfort food for the soul." Satellite provider DISH Network, cable provider Verizon FiOS, and Sling TV international live-streaming service all offer Italian language television programming, known as Rai Italia. This programming includes television series, variety shows, live news coverage, and sports channels. And if you're on the move, there's a handful of Rai radio apps, and other Italian radio apps, all providing a variety of Italian music, sports and news. Catch up on the latest Italian news stories or listen to soothing Italian opera broadcast via Rai apps.

No matter your proficiency or your schedule, there are many ways to improve your Italian language skills or to immerse yourself in culture.

SAINT ANTHONY'S FEAST

A few years ago, I'd experienced Saint Anthony's Feast in Boston's North End for the very first time. Growing up Italian in Buffalo, New York, I'd enjoyed summer Italian festivals before, as they're an annual fixture in most American cities. But nothing could prepare me for the sights and sounds of this, arguably the largest Italian festival in New England.

That day, my husband, Jamie, and I headed into Boston on the last weekend of August, when it's customarily held, with his grandmother, Josie, an eighty-five-year-old Italian immigrant whose wish it was to see the feast "one last time." Together we coaxed her wheelchair over the uneven sidewalks and cobblestone streets of the North End, toward the sound of parade music. Weaving through hordes of people of every ethnicity and age group, we halted abruptly at Endicott as church bells tolled noon, where, at that very moment, the Grand Procession passed. Josie grasped her rosary and recited prayers with the loveliest smile, her gaze following the statue of Saint Anthony of Padua, hoisted high in the air by devotees and trailed by marching bands, floats, and revelers. She wept, and I realized then that the Saint Anthony feast, celebrated every year here since 1919, is an extraordinarily meaningful tradition to Italians of faith in the community.

Saint Anthony of Padua, born in Portugal in 1195, was a Catholic priest and friar of the Franciscan order who died in 1231 in Padua, Italy. Noted for his forceful preaching and knowledge of scripture, he is the second most canonized saint, and the patron saint of finding lost items or people. My mom and her sisters recite the Prayer to Saint Anthony whenever they misplace something, whether an ordinary item like car keys, or even a valuable keepsake like a photograph, and in no time at all, it's almost always found.

The San Antonio di Padova da Montefalcione, Inc. is a nonprofit, religious and cultural organization founded in 1919 in Boston by a small group of Italian immigrants from the tiny mountain town of Montefalcione, Avellino, just east of Naples in Italy's Campania region. Their mission includes preserving Italian-American traditions, culture, history and heritage, and they are dedicated to continuing the tradition of the annual Saint Anthony's Feast in the North End of Boston. In the true spirit of their patron saint, they've supported many charities and organizations in the community and greater Boston, remembering those in need and assisting their fellow citizens.

Dubbed the "Feast of all Feasts" by *National Geographic*, the Italian street festival in Boston encompasses Endicott, Thacher, and North Margin Streets, where visitors may stroll beautifully decorated byways; taste some of the most delectable Italian street foods from over one hundred pushcarts, including cannoli, calamari, pizza, pasta, zeppole, and gelato; and experience daily live entertainment, contests, and religious services.

Boston's Saint Anthony's Feast is traditionally Friday-Sunday, the last weekend of August, with a bonus Santa Lucia Feast Day on the following Monday. In the past, the live shows and masses have always been free and open to the public, with donations accepted at the Chapel of Saint Anthony and Saint Lucy. The highlight of the event, the Grand Procession, begins at noon on Sunday and lasts ten hours. It's a cultural tradition that's not to be missed.

EXPRESSIVE ITALIANS

My friends can see me talking from a mile away, even with my back turned. I'm the one gesticulating in the air with my hands, sometimes with elegant precision as I speak on my cell phone, sometimes with wild abandon as I'm ordering a sandwich. That's because I was raised in an Italian household. Italians are typically expressive, passionate, and animated when communicating with others. It's a demonstration of engagement and interest. Have you ever seen an Italian converse with his or her hands in their pockets? Never happens.

Italians, young and old, male or female, gesture naturally. Whether they're busy licking a gelato, smoking a cigarette, or zipping a manual-shift car around a hilltop town, Italians are quite adept at pairing any activity with vivid hand gestures when engaged in conversation. Writing letters must drive most Italians crazy, as expression is limited. I regularly use emoticons when dashing off an email or posting on social media, because sometimes words are just not enough, and I feel happier using them. ;-)

Most people shake hands, but Italians typically grasp the other's arm at the same time. Eye contact is important to them, and so is close personal contact. In fact, once a relationship is established, a kiss on both cheeks upon greeting is the norm, even for an acquaintance. Public displays of affection among Italians are prevalent, both among couples and families. Sons and daughters are equally apt to hug and kiss their parents as a sign of respect and affection. Strolling arm and arm through Italian towns in companionship is practiced by neighbors and friends. Italian couples typically prefer a lip lock and tight embrace as further acknowledgment of their mutual affinity.

Americans, too, are known to gesture on occasion, such as a flipped bird (raised middle finger) during rush-hour traffic, pressed thumbs and knuckles in the shape of a heart from a mother to her child on the school bus, the peace sign

10

from a graduate accepting his diploma, or a thumbs-up to signal appreciation, among others.

Here are a few Italian gestures that might be fun to incorporate into everyday life:

- To gesture "Come here," instead of beckoning with an index finger, an Italian sweeps an entire arm downward.
- A beckoning index finger might signal a romantic enticement in both cultures. But in Italian culture, one might also do the same to signal that he or she wishes to convey something very important to another.
- Index fingers pressed against the thumbs with a slight waggle of both hands means an exasperated "What do you want from me?"
- The index finger twisted into the cheek means something is good, lovely, or tasty.
- Tapping one's wrist means "Hurry up."
- Two open hands stands for "What's happening here?"
- Waggling two hands pressed together as if in fervent prayer begs the question, "What do you want me to do about it?"
- The backside of one's fingers brushing the chin is a classic blow off, as in "Who gives a flying fig?"
- My grandfather used to pat his throat, and say *gola, gola*, meaning that he had chocolate candy or decadent cookies to share. And my nana would simply throw her arms wide, demonstrating the need for a grandchild's hug.

No matter the exuberant gesture or signal, Italians use them to enhance communication in an uninhibited, liberating way. Take it or leave it, we're just letting you know how passionate we are on a subject. <shrug and a smile>

HERITAGE, FRUGALITY OR BOTH?

Fall is harvest time, and it's then that I find myself squirreling away my food for the winter months ahead. Is it my Italian heritage, or a touch of frugality, or perhaps a little of both that spurs me to bottle, can, and store my family's food this time of year?

My family loves wine. We drink it with Sunday dinner, at family gatherings, and at many odd times in between. We own a wine store where we procure and sell fine wines from around the world. But the bottles of wine that my family drinks don't always come from the store. Instead, we make our own. Though we grow grapes on a small patch of land in our yard with a number of varietals, it's not enough juice to fill a bottle. Instead we buy a couple crates of grapes, press and ferment them, bottle them, and drink the delicious product. My husband, a Master of Italian Wine, finds wine-making therapeutic. I enjoy drinking it. But the whole process fills me with nostalgia.

When my grandfather came to America, he too made wine. With the bushels of grapes he'd buy from the Clinton Market, he'd smash grapes in his cellar every fall. My younger brothers and I loved the aroma that emanated from my grandparents' home in Buffalo, New York. Our heads would swim with the musty fermentation of huge aged barrels filled with gallons of red wine. And every Sunday, my grandmother would spike our ginger ale over Sunday pasta. This is the joy of making your own.

My grandparents also handed down to us the art of curing prosciutto. Nana would pull the salt-cured leg of pork from a cold, dark spare closet where she hid all the grandkids' treats (like Snickers, Oreos, and Nutella.) My nana would hold the massive pork leg against her apron-clad chest, and with the oldest and sharpest knife she owned, she'd carve for us paper-thin, melt-in-your-mouth slices of prosciutto. My father, brothers, and husband likewise hang cured prosciutto in their dark, cold basements for impromptu picnic sandwiches.

And the bread! There's nothing like walking into a home that smells of rising yeast, kneaded dough, and just-baked loaves of bread. In my opinion, there's never been a better comfort food than bread, unless it's some derivation like pizza, pretzels, or calzones.

Every year, my father plants his garlic in the spring and pulls the gigantic bulbs from the earth in the fall. He braids each plant together into one long rope, and my mother plucks from its bounty of garlic for all sorts of recipes all year.

Of course, like the garlic, the same goes for the vegetables that we pull from our gardens. We use them until the crop runs out. But what do we do with the excess bounty? Can it, bottle it, store it. The full length of my grandparents' basement was lined with wooden doors that my grandfather built to house shelf upon shelf of jarred peaches (where the syrup ran down your chin and wrists as you slurped them from the jar), canned tomatoes (used to make sauce all year through), and other assorted novelties like pickled eggs or cucumbers, or even pickled pigs' feet.

There's something to be said for all the money my frugal grandparents and parents saved by squirreling away food for the winter. They put all their kids through college and spent wonderful years spoiling their grandchildren during retirement. But the art of preserving one's food isn't lost on my generation. I hope to hand it down to my children. It's not just the art of preserving nourishment, but it's the nourishing act of preserving one's own heritage that feeds the soul.

ITALIAN CULTURAL ORGANIZATIONS: A GATHERING OF PAESANI

As an author of mystery novels that are set in Italy, I truly enjoy sharing stories with my some of my biggest fans, Italian-Americans. Where do I go to connect with some of my most loyal readers? Italian cultural organizations are typically nonprofit groups that meet monthly with the objective of promoting Italian language and culture, and preserving Italian heritage, within a local community.

I'm often contacted by Italian cultural groups to speak to their members and guests about many of the juicy tidbits that make it into my novels, such as Italian geography, car racing, culture, history, food, wine, politics, celebrities, and family life. But I've found that I learn a great deal more from my audience than I could ever imagine, like cannoli recipes, genealogy, DIY outdoor projects, fashion ideas, art exhibits, and much more.

One of the pleasures of these face-to-face social gatherings is the camaraderie between those who share similar values and interests. Of course, when all of these *paesani* are in one room, it's a chance to break bread, drink wine, laugh, and enjoy lengthy conversations spoken in Italian. It's a gathering of like-minded individuals and families who leave behind their busy routine to meet regularly and share special moments with old and new friends alike.

At such a meeting, the president of the organization typically runs the agenda, and various committees report future plans. Social events might include a regional winery or olive oil factory tour, a visit to a local museum, a night at the opera, a visit to a saint's feast day celebration, a dinner at a local Italian restaurant, a bocce tournament, or a Christmas party. Groups often host annual extravaganzas featuring community artisans, vendors, and performers. In-house speakers might include authors, pastry chefs, singers, and painters. Fundraisers might feature fashion shows or a local concert, all with the idea of funding the scholarship committee, who annually present a monetary award to a local high school student. Such activities, field trips, and speakers all take place with the

14

objective of promoting a sense of community and preserving heritage among Italians in a town or city.

Young and old, members of a group often include single individuals looking to forge new friendships, as well as whole families seeking to develop bonds with their neighbors. It's a great way to network business relationships, find a reliable babysitter, or hire a professional for a house project. And why not join multiple groups and expand the network of friends across a local region, or even in different parts of the country, while staying in touch via Facebook, text, email, and Skype?

There are hundreds, if not thousands, of Italian cultural organizations across the country, both local and national. Browse online or call a local Italian consulate to learn more. Here are just a few:

- National Order of the Sons of Italy
- Dante Alighieri Society
- Friends of the Italian Cultural Society
- The Pirandello Lyceum
- Associazione Lucchesi nel Mondo
- Appian Club
- Associazione Amici
- St. Joseph Society
- Italia Unita

Hope to see you there!

MOLTO SUPERSTITIOUS

I remember my grandmother's panicked reaction to my nearly knocking a large mirror from a wall as a child. It wasn't the physical injury or even the cleanup that she'd feared most had it shattered to the floor. She was afraid of what might become of her granddaughter's fate, doomed with seven long years of bad luck that would surely ensue from a broken mirror. When it happened, my nana set the mirror aside, hugged me tight, wiped the nervous perspiration from her nose, and walked me to her kitchen to find something sweet to eat, muttering prayers of thanks to God for saving me. I'll never forget it.

Italian culture is rich with superstitions, both good and evil, and many of them pervade everyday life. Some superstitions are rooted in ancient history, based on religious beliefs or communal rites. Others were spawned and passed on simply to encourage prosperity or to discourage strife. No matter their derivation, most of them carry on throughout generations, as it may be safer to believe in them than not.

Here is a list of the most commonly held Italian superstitions, along with a handful mixed in that my family has uniquely observed. Take a moment to consider your own routines, and you just might find that time-honored superstitions influence your family's behavior.

Lucky and Unlucky Numbers

The number 13 is lucky in Italy. Unlike Americans who are wary of it, especially on Friday the 13th, in Italy the number is thought to bring prosperity and abundant life. My father and brothers all wear a thin chain of gold around their necks bearing a lucky number 13, which they never remove.

On the contrary, Italians take heed of the unlucky Friday the 17th. When 17 is written in Arabic numerals, it represents a man hanging from a noose. When written in Roman numerals, XVII, it's an anagram of VIXI, meaning "I have lived" in Latin; once inscribed on ancient tombstones, the word is thought to tempt death.

The Evil Eye (*Malocchio*)

The Evil Eye, thought to be a curse cast upon one by another bearing envy or jealousy, is an ancient superstition but still carries significant weight. My husband's grandmothers both recited prayers before bed to ward off any possible malocchio cast upon members of their families. The curse was generally thought to be one of ill tidings wrought upon a person or household, but many conceive it to mean a curse against one's "manliness." In other words, if a man was cursed by the evil eye, his potency was in jeopardy, and he ran the risk of his lover straying. Aside from grandma's prayers, there's another remedy against malocchio…

The Devil's Horn (*Corno*)

The Devil's Horn, or corno, is a twisted phallic amulet worn by a man to ward off curses on his manliness. Related to this is the hand gesture known as the mano cornuta, where one extends the pinkie and index finger upwards, to curse another or to imply that another's mojo has been compromised. Pointed down, the gesture wards off the curse.

Good Omens

- Itchy palms are a sign that one will soon come into some money.
- If you drop a fork or a spoon, unexpected company will soon pay a visit.
- Gift a new broom to newlyweds, for sweeping away evil spirits from a new home; salt sprinkled in the corners of the dwelling will also serve to purify it.
- If you gift someone a wallet or purse, always put a coin in it.
- It's good luck to hear a cat sneeze.

- Spotting a spider at night signals an impending windfall.
- Finding a button signals a new friendship is coming.
- Throw your cracked dishes and worn pots and pans out into the driveway/street to ring in the New Year, as in "out with the old and in with the new," ensuring prosperity and vitality in the year to come. (This custom/superstition is one my grandparents brought with them from Italy and passed along to my parents. Though interesting and fun, I've never heard of it elsewhere.)
- Another New Year superstition is eating green grapes and a shot of Sambuca at the stroke of midnight, also ensuring prosperity through the new year, also passed on from my grandparents and parents, and also unique.

Bad Omens

- Don't spill salt or olive oil for fear of bad luck. If you do, toss a pinch a salt over your left shoulder, or rub a dab of oil behind each ear.
- Never open an umbrella inside the house, which is also bad luck.
- Never gift anything sharp (scissors, knives, or a hatchet) as the giver may later endure hardship.
- Do not gift white lilies to an elderly person, as this surely hastens his or her demise.
- A loaf of bread must always be placed faceup, or else one may suffer the wrath of God.
- Birds in the house bring bad luck (either in the form of a pet, an accidental entry, mere feathers, or even a painting.)
- A single person should never let a broom touch his feet when another is sweeping, or else he will never be swept off his feet and therefore never marry.
- It's bad luck to let a black cat cross your path.

- Never put a hat on the bed because, hearkening back to the times when a priest would remove his hat upon calling on a sick bed, it invites illness, sleeplessness, or death.
- Never place a bed to face the door, as it's reminiscent of a coffin in a church.
- Never raise a toast with a glass of water, and don't cross arms when clinking wineglasses.
- Never follow an empty hearse, as you are riding in death's wake. But, you're safe if the hearse is already carrying a coffin.
- Killing a spider is bad luck.
- Never trim your nails on a Thursday.
- Never start a journey or get married on a Friday or Tuesday.
- Be careful never to break a mirror, as it guarantees seven years of bad luck.

While the above superstitions are the most common or endearing to me, the list is surely limitless. Also, I feel pretty confident about killing a big, hairy spider any day of the week, as the consequences of keeping it alive would surely be worse. So, be sure to take these with a grain of salt (over your left shoulder.)

While Italian superstitions may seem strange or silly to some, our family, like so many others, embraces them as another way to immerse ourselves in our culture and to connect with other generations. In doing so, *tocca ferro* (touch iron, as the Italians do), we hope to benefit from an abundance of *buona fortuna*! Good luck!

PURSUITS

BOCCE, ANYONE?

Bocce is a competitive sport, a strategic game, and a leisurely pastime, all rolled into one ever-popular activity. The object is to roll balls on a court as close to a target ball as possible to score points. Dating back to the Roman Empire, bocce, in all its derivations, has since captured the hearts of players and spectators the world over, no matter their age or skill level. And, if you peek into some of the backyards or parking lots of local hangouts across America, it seems the popularity of bocce has shifted into high gear.

I have fond memories of running through my grandparents' backyard as a young girl, tossing the tiny white pallina through the freshly mown grass of summer while the adults chased after it with their teams' heavier, larger red or green balls in hopes of scoring points during a weekend pickup game in my mostly Italian neighborhood in South Buffalo, New York. Friends and neighbors would join in on the fun all day, some recounting how they used to play in their local piazze back in Italy. It was a chance to be together, and to catch up on each other's lives. And no matter how old you were, it was an opportunity to just play outside with your friends.

My husband did the same thing as a kid living north of Boston. So, a few years ago, when my parents gave us a bocce set for Christmas, we decided to carve out a corner of our own yard for a court. When the ground thawed, we hooked some railroad ties together with rebar, and we spread some stone dust on a scrap of yard under some trees—instant bocce court! (Here's a link on how to build your own court and how to play: http://www.wikihow.com/Play-Bocce-Ball.) Now, every summer we pull up a few lawn chairs for our family, neighbors, and friends, and we roll out some fun. Our children are outside, getting fresh air and exercise, enjoying friendly competition with their buddies—they think it's cool. Who am I to tell them it's old-fashioned?

Actually, it's very cool these days. While bocce is still a regular fixture at many senior centers and public parks, now bars and restaurants are sacrificing parking space and rooftop accommodations for bocce courts because the demand is so high. Move over darts and billiards, bocce's in town.

The United States Bocce Federation, or USBC, was established in 1977 and is the preeminent organization that sets the rules, promotes the sport, and establishes guidelines for players on the countrywide and international levels. The US Bocce National Championships, first held in Las Vegas in 1979, roll around the country every year. In 2015, the event was held for the first time ever in New England, when the Methuen Sons of Italy, Lodge 902, hosted over one hundred and fifty elite bocce players in five different events over the course of the week. If you think you've got what it takes to compete with the best, or if you simply want to join in on the fun of watching the best, be sure to check it out at the USBC website. In addition, Major League Bocce is an organization, founded in 2004, that promotes bocce leagues for sport and fun across the country. Check out their website or Facebook page for locations around the country.

Bocce's come a long way, and now, more than ever, it appears that future generations are guiding it along to a thriving tomorrow. Perhaps soon, "Bocce, anyone?" will become just as likely an invitation as any other.

STUDY ABROAD IN ITALY

In the nineties, I studied abroad during college, traveling to Italy with the intention of chalking up credits in international business. But my experiences reached way beyond grades. I met new people, including my husband, immersed myself in the culture, became fluent in Italian, and hopped trains all over Italy and the rest of Europe at every opportunity. It was the experience of a lifetime and one that fueled my desire to explore further. My time studying abroad loosely shaped the story of Mara Silvestri, the main character in my suspense novel, *The Sculptor*, a grad student who's stalked by Rome's infamous serial killer. Subsequent visits back to the Eternal City influenced my thrillers *The Race*, in which a car-racing covert agent must save Rome from a terrorist from his past, and *Formula*, in which my race car driver returns to investigate a winery after a rival's fatal poisoning.

Recently, my daughter, Sabrina, studied abroad in Rome during her freshman year of college. The challenge of diving headfirst into the college experience while living in a foreign country was daunting at first, but it soon unfolded into an exhilarating adventure. She gained friendships, independence, street smarts, and a bit of gumption that will surely last a lifetime. When our family visited her, it was clear that her younger brother, Mario, had succumbed to the infectious desire to explore international studies in the future.

But the predeparture planning stages differ markedly between the nineties, when Jamie and I had organized our own study trips, and the present day, when Sabrina planned hers. Today's environment includes far more stringent visa requirements, but extremely helpful online resources. The sections that I outline below represent firsthand advice for students and parents interested in seeking a global view during the college years.

A Checklist

As soon as a student expresses interest in studying abroad, it's important to begin preparation early. Here's a checklist of the key steps in the process:

- Apply for or renew your passport. Do it soon, as processing may take three to nine months. Once it arrives, make a copy of the photo page to keep with you but separate from your passport, and another to leave behind with family in case of theft.
- Research colleges, countries, and courses online, and also visit a study abroad office at a local college or a local consulate.

- Contact institutions of interest for their curricula to narrow down choice of university and program and gather their requisite applications.
- Compile your academic portfolio. Organize transcripts, gather letters of recommendation, and write personal essays and curricula vitae.
- Organize pertinent financial information, such as bank statements, loan documents, and tax returns, if choosing to apply for any financial aid.
- Once a student selects a university, complete all applications and forms, including admissions, financial aid, housing, and health forms.
- Research and obtain any visas applicable to the university country.
- Make arrangements for appropriate health insurance coverage, for illness or accident. Address any health needs in advance (allergies or asthma medications, vaccinations, contact lenses, feminine needs, etc.)
- Schedule preparatory classes and orientations. Attend any local orientation sessions that will ease the burden of logistics. Sign up for prerequisite courses at local community colleges to enhance your major.
- Learn the language and the culture. (More on this later.)
- Chat online with study-abroad students who've been through the process and have studied or are studying in the host country, for advice that might range from packing, traveling, and coping with homesickness all the way to ideas for places to eat, visit, or shop. There are many online forums where international students gather and provide advice.
- Book airline reservations, preferably well in advance to take advantage of the best pricing and options.
- Prepare your spending money. Convert some cash to the local currency before you go, in case you're hungry or need a cab or need to place a call and a bank holiday prevents conversion on the day you arrive. If you plan to use a credit card for any expenses, be sure to apply for one

now and familiarize yourself with the host country's ATM fee policy and cash advance limits.

- Pack. At the very least, get a suitcase with wheels and an everyday backpack. Don't forget to buy adapters and converters for chargers, technology, and appliances (hair dryers, etc.) based on Italian specifications and those of any countries to which the student plans to travel.

Choosing Where to Go

The decision of where to study abroad in Italy can be a daunting process. Here are some topics to consider when narrowing your search for a city and a host school, your home away from home for the duration.

Language

Though Italy is primarily an Italian-speaking country, many of its natives speak English. Getting along in everyday life is relatively easy. However, one of the reasons a student may choose to study in Italy is to become fluent in the Italian language, so taking on the challenge of immersing in the culture can be a gratifying goal. Still, most host colleges and universities there that team with an American counterpart will offer lectures and testing in English.

Course of Study and Logistics

Do the educational institutions on your short list offer programs in your desired field of study? Do they match your time table—semester, year, graduate term? Do the internships or job opportunities offered there appeal to you the most? What is the cost of tuition, fees, and room and board in the cities/colleges under top consideration? What are the visa requirements, and can they be met?

Culture and Environment

Learning firsthand the history, politics, and economics of a region's culture is another consideration. If you are an art major, for example, consider those cities renowned for their worldwide impact, like Rome or Florence. Also, consider whether a big city like Milan is right for you or if more rural settings, like Siena, appeal to your sensibilities.

International Scholarships

International scholarships may cover tuition, tuition fees, living expenses, travel costs, and/or insurance costs. There are a variety of scholarships, grants, fellowships, prizes, competitions, and awards available, based on merit and/or background. There are a number of online resources designed to narrow down the search based on nationality, host institution, course study, need, and/or merit, including:

- http://www.internationalstudent.com/scholarships
- http://www.scholarshipportal.eu/

The Transition from "Culture Shock" to "Cultural Adventure"

One of the main objectives in deciding to pursue international studies is to gain an appreciation of the new culture, including differences in language, cuisine, mode of transportation, style of dress, music, and a host of other concepts. But for some, the shock of cultural absorption may be overwhelming. It's natural and common to experience a bit of anxiety in exploring the unknown, but the key is to funnel that culture shock into a cultural adventure. Before long, what feels strange will become familiar.

The mix of emotions that one experiences may include loss, fatigue, stress, anxiety, and confusion. Some degree of culture shock is inevitable, and the range of emotions at any given time typically transition through four stages: 1) the honeymoon stage; 2) the frustration phase; 3) depression/isolation stage; and 4) adjustment and acceptance phase. Awareness of these stages may help

26

alleviate the issue and provide a smoother path to the final stage. As long as one lives the cultural transition fully rather than resisting this normal phenomenon, the experience will feel much more positive, much sooner. What you learn will soon become a part of you, adding worldliness to your character that will reap lifelong benefits. Here are some valuable methods for easing into the cultural adventure:

Learn the language now, and later.

Sign up for local, short-term language immersion classes, or longer-term classroom study to enhance conversation. There are also a number of home computer programs, like Rosetta Stone, and apps, like Duolingo, Babel and iTranslate, that will assist preparation for the trip and aid assimilation once you've arrived.

Learn the culture, and use it.

Practice cooking Italian food or visit local restaurants. Listen to Italy's popular music. Live-stream the country's popular TV shows. Research the lesser-known historic and artistic gems and become well versed in the popular ones.

Chat online with study abroad students.

Contact others who've been through the process and have studied or are studying there, for advice that might range from packing, traveling, and coping with homesickness, all the way to ideas for places to eat, visit, or shop. There are many on-line forums where international students gather and provide advice.

Achieve a Balance - embrace the adventure but stay true to one's self.

Once there, try new cuisine on a regular basis, but when you're feeling blue, offset it with a visit to your favorite fast-food chain or cook up something that you'd normally fix at home. Pick up a local trinket or don clothing that reflects the local custom, but take some time to revel in the items you bring from home, like photos, a teddy bear, or a favorite sweater. Attend music performances that typically reside outside your genre, but keep your favorite tunes plugged in on your way to class. Learn to bike ride through traffic or hillsides, but walk or grab a taxi when the mood moves you. Join a club or volunteer to become a part of the society around you, but feel free to kick back with a newspaper about home. In other words, balance the challenge with a taste of home.

Get by with a Little Help from Your Friends and Family.

Don't underestimate the power of companionship. Whether you seek the tutelage of a professor, the commonality of a roommate with a similar background, or even a brand new group of classmates, it's important to stay connected. Share your experiences, and you just might learn a few things. Also, meeting locals is a great way to immerse in the culture, and they may end up friends in which to visit or correspond long after you've returned home, or otherwise contacts in which to network should you extend your stay. And finally, stay in touch with those back home. They will boost your morale, and keep you grounded during those times when you're a little tired of spreading your wings. Upon return, sharing your adventure will be more meaningful if others have stayed abreast of your ongoing activity while you're away.

Consider my daughter Sabrina's wisdom on the subject. She said, "It's the experience of a lifetime that gave me a lifetime of experience."

THE MOVIE THEATER EXPERIENCE

Ah, going to the movies…the big screen, the packed seats, the emotional highs and lows of a great film, the whispers of "whodunit?," the couples holding hands, and the wafting aroma of…marinara sauce?

One of the pleasures of Italy is going to the movies. It's an experience all its own. I love movies, and while studying in Rome in the 90's, most weekends I'd frequent a movie house in the Trastevere neighborhood. "Il Pasquino" showed American movies, typically ones I'd already seen, but it was a great taste of home.

My first time at Il Pasquino was the most memorable, because I had no idea just how different movie theaters in Italy are from those in America. My boyfriend at the time (now my husband, Jamie,) and I bought tickets at the entrance, and then we settled into our seats for a showing of *Balla Coi Lupi* (Dances with Wolves.) Typical screen and typical seats, that's where the similarities ended. While waiting for the projector to start rolling (yes, I'm dating myself,) an elderly couple showed us their tickets and told us we were sitting in their seats. Assigned seats? Apparently, Italian cinemas are big on assigned seating at most movie theaters, to this day.

After we cozied into our new seats, the movie rolled, and I can tell you, Kevin Costner never sounded so good. That's because even though the movie was in English, Costner's voice was dubbed over by an Italian voice actor, known as a *doppiaggio*. This dubbing practice is prevalent, even today, and Italian cinema and television prides itself on its voice actors, who usually follow the real actor's movie journey throughout his or her career. A funny side note: it's tricky making a movie featuring both DeNiro and Pacino as they're both dubbed by the same voice actor (which would present an interesting viewing of *The Godfather*!)

Jamie and I soon got used to the Costner stand-in and enjoyed the movie. That is, until the smell of marinara wafting in from the lobby made our stomachs growl. We'd both seen the movie before, and we decided to wait until after a major scene to dash out to the lobby for a bite. But just as the character named "Stands with a Fist" so intimately shares conversation with her handsome male lead, the film stopped, mid-scene, with a frame that read "Intervallo" (intermission!) Then and now, Italians stop their movies mid-way, regardless of the artistic timing, and grant their patrons about five minutes of freedom to move about the theater or to chat with friends on their opinion of the film thus far. Before Jamie and I could dash to the lobby to surmise the source of the aromatic sauce, a concessionaire toting a box strapped around his neck, similar to a sporting event, began selling bags of popcorn, chips, and soda. On subsequent visits to Il Pasquino, I did determine the root of the saucy aroma - the lobby sold hot food too: *arancini* or *suppli* (breaded orange-size balls of rice and mozzarella, with marinara sauce for dipping,) as well as eggplant and zucchini fritters, among other delectable munchies.

Today, the overall experience remains the same in many Italian cinemas: assigned seating, dubbed voice actors, intermission, halftime concession, and diverse food offerings.

The interior design of an Italian movie theater is similar to that of an American one. The difference lies in the exterior: Italian ones are usually smaller, more intimate, local one-screen playhouses in each community, whereas American movie theaters are often times multiscreen megaplexes. Italians seem to prefer the experience of the smaller playhouse, though Cinecity megaplexes are sprouting in bigger cities up north. If you're headed to Italy, here's a great link for finding a cinema near you: http://www.cinematreasures.org/theaters/italy.

I've experienced similar experiences here in the States at local art houses and independent cinemas, intimate theaters that show current mainstream films as well as throwback-era gems, independent films, documentaries, and foreign classics.

On a recent visit to my hometown of Buffalo, I enjoyed an evening viewing of *Life Is Beautiful*, an Academy-award winning Italian film by Roberto Benigni, in the historic and recently renovated North Park Theatre, a richly detailed single-screen theater with an Art Deco marquee and an ornate interior that exudes warmth and nostalgia, lending to the viewing experience.

Boston and surrounding towns also feature a wealth of renowned cinemas, including these fan favorites:

- Brattle Theatre, a single-screen gem in Harvard Square since 1953;
- Somerville Theatre, a five-screener that serves beer and wine and occasionally hosts concerts;
- Kendall Square Cinema, which boasts a parking garage and some of the best popcorn around, along with documentaries and foreign flicks galore; and
- Coolidge Corner Theatre, in the heart of Brookline, serving beer, wine, ice cream, and popcorn topped with real butter.

No matter your taste in film, the time of year, or what town you live in, it's always the perfect time to go to the movies…with or without the marinara.

BROWSING ITALIAN BOOKSTORES

What could be better than strolling the aisles of a bookstore? Choose a selection from among hundreds of books. Balance the weight of a hard- or softcover volume in your hand. Sniff the paper as you turn the pages, and listen to the sheets softly ruffle with ample promise beneath your fingertips. Know that the gem in your hand represents something akin to the mystery of turning wine into blood, or rather ink into imagination?

I enjoy perusing bookstores, a pastime that's both emotionally comforting and mentally stimulating at the same time. I love poking my head into

31

bookshops no matter where I go—whether in my hometown, while visiting a neighboring locale, or when traveling to a distant land. For me, there's something about it that grounds me when I'm far from home, but that transports me when I'm shopping locally.

When I studied in Rome during college, the gargantuan chain store La Feltrinelli in Piazza della Repubblica near Termini station was a no-brainer stop-off for something to read before hopping a train on the weekend. Stephen King novels were my go-to books of choice back then, and I picked up my copies of *The Stand*, *It*, and King's collection of Bachman books there. The multilingual chain is still huge throughout Italy, and those books still reside on my bookshelf.

My husband, Jamie, who lived in Trastevere during college, introduced me to his favorite bookstore in that neighborhood, Open Door Bookshop. It's a family-run independent bookstore that has been around a long time, and it's chock full of secondhand books. It's the only used bookshop in all of Rome, and the inventory rotates regularly, so it's worth checking out.

A couple years ago, while Jamie spent a day wine-tasting in Verona for work, I spent the day in a little piazza near Juliet's balcony, sifting through Italian and English titles at a lovely bookstore there. I cozied up in a chair for a couple of hours with an Italian version and an English-translated copy of Dante's *Divine Comedy*, devouring the classic while improving my understanding of the Italian language. I did the same with a Patricia Cornwall novel and a book on soccer, leaving no genre unturned. I highly recommend this fruitful learning experience of soaking up literature, culture, and language while juxtaposing both versions of a title.

I recommend hunting down an Italian bookstore in any major city. Most are the embodiment of a cultural adventure, serving as both a bookstore with titles for children and adults in both English and Italian and a hub for musicians, authors, and artists to share their passion with the community.

LONG-DISTANCE GRANDPARENTS: BRIDGING THE DISTANCE

While it's not uncommon these days for people to find that many miles on a road map, or even a world map, separate their kids from their grandparents, it's also easier than ever before to minimize that distance by incorporating some easy techniques for bringing the generations closer in heart and mind.

Travel Together

Planning and partaking in a family vacation, reunion, or outing can sometimes rejuvenate familial bonds, or just provide another excuse for getting together. Whether it's a daylong family reunion, a fun meeting spot between states, or a leisurely travel destination, an occasional trip provides a welcome retreat. The preparation and post-vacation photos may provide just as many enduring memories.

Getting away is a great opportunity for inspiring life lessons and history, too. A few years back, my parents joined me and my family on a trip to Italy, where my dad was born, and we traced the paths he walked as a child. My children learned about their *nonno*'s roots, and those roots became theirs.

Share Traditions

Friends of mine who live out-of-state often hop in the car and drive nearly seven hundred miles, especially at Christmastime, to share a lovely tradition of watching *The Polar Express* with their two young grandsons. Together, they all read a favorite book called *The Night Tree* and then decorate an evergreen with food for woodland creatures.

Communicate via Technology

Staying connected during the time spent apart is easy to do with technology. Don't know how? Ask your grandchild. They know technology better than anyone, so why not ask for a few lessons?

Chat regularly, and face-to-face, with Skype, ooVoo, or Facetime. Converse anytime, anywhere, in real time. Technology allowed our family in Massachusetts to watch a relative's wedding ceremony take place in Tuscany, while it was happening. Email and social media play a big part in helping long-distance grandparents stay connected, too. Copy and email a report card, recipe, or sports score; post pictures on Facebook, or tweet funny jokes; download a video game app on a tablet or phone and compete, or play together split-screen online with game consoles. Join an online fantasy sports league. Join an online book club via Skype.

Communicate the Old-Fashioned Way

Staying connected the old-fashioned way (picking up the phone to chat) works just as well. No need for an excuse; just call and tell him or her that you love them.

Here are a few other ideas:

- Write a letter, slip a silly note into a care package, or mail some pictures.
- Get crafty, and then mail it.
- Journal back and forth through the mail.
- Send fun or educational postcards from travels.
- Regularly gift grandchildren a disposable camera for snapping random shots of their life, giving you insight into a child's perspective.

Learn to Adapt

Generations sometimes find it difficult to reach each other on common ground, no matter the age or the distance. Long-distance grandparents must learn to adapt.

These days, my mom still sings a lullaby to her younger grandchildren just as sweetly as she did with me and my brothers. But their nana also tunes in to her older grandkids' musical tastes on occasion, so that they have something to chat about over the phone.

Grandparents are also invaluable mentors, especially while participating in a shared activity, like baking, painting, or canoeing. Exploring books, movies, television shows, and art together may yield surprising common affinities. Read or view them in tandem, and compare notes in real time or during an upcoming visit.

Maybe it's not what you talk about that brings you closer, but the activities you share:

- If there are games, there are families having fun together. Pull out a deck of cards, deal out a hand of Scopa, and have fun.
- Make the most of whatever the nearest big city has to offer when they visit.
- Explore the grandchild's state's attractions.
- Attend church together.
- Make pasta with the older kids, or roll pretzels with the younger ones.
- Fly kites in the backyard.
- Volunteer in a child's classroom when you visit.
- Work on tandem projects from afar (a birdhouse, a recipe, a garden, etc.) and then snap photos of each other's progress to share.
- Plant a tree in the backyard together, and watch the tree, and children, grow.

35

For long-distance grandparents and their grandchildren, it's the time spent together, near or far, with moments captured of one-on-one conversation that is most valuable, so plan for it, make it happen whenever possible, and cherish every minute of it.

A TRIP TO THE MUSEUM

My teenage daughter once returned from a school field trip to Boston's Museum of Fine Arts, frustrated by the short amount of time they had to appreciate the abundant artwork on display there. One day soon, we're going back. For a full day, or maybe a bunch of them. Why not take a moment for a museum retreat, either solo or with family and friends? No matter the season, it's always a good time to explore the sculptures, paintings, tapestries, and decorative pieces showcased in a local museum. There are masterpieces found around every corner, very reminiscent of Italy's museums.

Italy has a wide array of world-renowned museums, like the Uffizi in Florence, home to Botticelli's *Birth of Venus*; the Vatican museums, which house a treasure trove of pieces and artifacts; or Rome's Sistine Chapel, where craning one's neck permits optimal viewing of Michelangelo's famed ceiling. But there are also lesser-known Italian venues that boast equally impressive works, like Rome's Church of St. Peter in Vincoli, featuring the tomb of Cardinal Cinzio Passeri Aldobrandini, decorated with bold, lifelike imagery of the Grim Reaper, which happens to grace the cover of my novel *The Sculptor*. Visit the Naval Museum in Venice, where relics and artistry tell the tales of Venice's tumultuous naval history. My son loved the life-sized ship replicas there. And nearly every town that dots the Tuscan hills features its own museum of wine-making and Etruscan relics. Throughout Italy, museums abound.

As a child, my father and I were told not to miss Michelangelo's *David* in Florence. When we saw the statue's full-sized splendor outside in the Piazza della Signoria, the gateway to the Uffizi Gallery, we had no idea that it was a mere replica of the original sculpture, which was moved from the piazza in 1873 and displayed inside the Accademia Gallery to protect it from damage. The replica is beautiful, but the original marble depiction of the Bible's David is breathtaking. Just don't visit on a Monday, when the Accademia is closed, or you'll be relegated to the outdoor version. Also, to avoid the long lines, try to string a few days together and enjoy a couple hours every late afternoon. Or if you're like many who line up in the morning, bring snacks and a museum guidebook to plot your route through the galleries while you wait. The bars surrounding the major museums often disallow bathroom breaks, so be prepared to scout public WCs and take turns holding your spot in line with friends.

Closer to home for me in Boston, the Museum of Fine Arts (MFA) is rich with Italian works, among them are paintings by such masters as Duccio, Fra Angelico, Botticelli, and Titian. These are complemented by sculptural works such as Donatello's *Madonna of the Clouds*, his only piece found in America; the bronze *Bust of Cleopatra* by the sculptor Pier Jacopo Alari Bonacolsi; and many others found in the Italian Renaissance Gallery. Just down the road at the Isabella Stewart Gardner Museum, Renaissance artwork abounds, including a room devoted entirely to Raphael's work.

My hometown, Buffalo, boasts the famous Albright-Knox Art Gallery, a major showplace for modern and contemporary art works that's listed in the National Register of Historic Places. The gallery's collection includes pieces spanning several centuries by artists such as Vincent van Gogh, Pablo Picasso, Henri Matisse, Jackson Pollock, and Andy Warhol. In 1978, one of the gallery's exhibitions was chosen to represent the United States at the 28th Venice Biennale. In 1988, the museum again won the competition to represent the United States in Venice.

Whether a museum trip takes you across the ocean or down the street, there's plenty of artwork to behold. Whether your day of art appreciation takes you to a church, a courtyard, or a museum, venues typically host exhibitions of historic and contemporary art, as well as concerts, lectures, and family and community programs. Take time to enrich your soul with the splendor of artistic creations.

VINITALY: FOR THE LOVE OF WINE…AND VERONA

Wine lovers know that one of the best times to travel to Italy is fall harvest season, when vineyards are ripe with the taste of bountiful production and just-uncorked reds and whites at roadside stands, called *enoteche*, beckon to be tasted. But why wait for fall for great wine-tasting adventures? A major springtime event gathers renowned Italian vintners eager to show off the fruits of their labor, all under one roof.

Vinitaly, also known as the International Wine & Spirits Exhibition, is the biggest, the oldest, and arguably the most popular wine convention in the world, held every April since 1967 in glorious Verona, Italy. It's a veritable Monte Carlo Grand Prix for established wine producers, a place for them to really rev their engines and show what's under the hood. It's also a proving ground for up-and-coming vintners akin to the Indianapolis 500, where a good showing here might mean a shot at a long run. For distributors and wholesalers, it's a place to determine which wines and spirits will sell big that year. Vintners woo restaurateurs, caterers, and wine store owners with their wares, while the world's journalists and opinion leaders take note. At Vinitaly, tourists aren't just spectators; they're participants in the biggest wine and spirits tasting event of the year.

A few years back, I accompanied my resident sommelier and Master of Italian Wines, my husband, Jamie, to Vinitaly. But what I'd thought was a business trip turned out to be an adventure. The event kicks off on Saturday night with a stunning wine bar event open to the public, sponsored by the international trade fair's organizer, Veronafiere, and is held in the historic center of Verona, in the alluring setting of the Palazzo della Gran Guardia in Piazza Bra. With Verona's colossal amphitheater as a backdrop, the gala is but a starting point to an evening that spills into the restaurants and upscale boutiques lining the piazza and rambles down the marbled main thoroughfare, Via Mazzini, home to Gucci, Prada, Furla, and Cartier. And that's just the welcome wagon.

For the next three days, the Vinitaly complex bustles, with over one hundred and fifty thousand visitors per year. Just outside the stone walls of Verona's city proper, the exhibition spreads over ninety-five thousand square meters and showcases themed tastings of more than four thousand exhibitors in various buildings dedicated to the official regions of Italy. Our particular wine-tasting itinerary sampled offerings from the finest producers, such as Cecchi, Banfi, Sartori, Villa Sandi, and Marchesi de' Frescobaldi, to name a few. Jamie and I sipped, swished, and spat some of the finest vintages, such as Sassicaia, Nero d'Avola, Amarone, and Franciacorto, along with better-known varietals such as Pinot Grigio, Prosecco, Montepulciano d'Abruzzo, and Brunello di Montalcino. At tables built into propped castles and fashionable bars, the bejeweled and Armani-clad vintners dazzled us with history and production methods while Jamie scribbled copious notes about acidity, tannins, and carbonic maceration, all Greek to me but critical in his business decisions. We'd chat with vineyard representatives for close to an hour, and then we'd elbow our way through open-air corridors ripe with the aroma of sweet grapes, cured meats, aged cheese, and high-priced perfume until we arrived at the next bountiful spread. For me, the event introduced me to rare and complex wines in which I'd otherwise never gain access.

Every day at Vinitaly is an education, a spectator sport, and a delicious carnival, all rolled into one. Just when the day seems to squeeze the last bit of energy from a weary traveler, a brief respite at any one of the fine hotels dotting the city center or the convention roadway handily smooths over the edges. After that, nighttime inside Verona's walls awaits.

Shakespeare wrote, "There is no world without Verona walls, but purgatory, torture, hell itself..." Verona is home to one of the best preserved Roman amphitheaters in the world. Built in AD 30, it features plays, opera and modern concerts to a capacity of fifteen thousand during the summer months. But, the lights stay on all year, and during Vinitaly, they appear extra bright. Also of note—Juliet's balcony, the setting for one of Shakespeare's best known plays. Lovers can sign their names or tuck a love letter into Juliet's Wall, which leads into the small piazza bearing her statue, whose right breast is worn from decades of luck-seekers.

Shops and restaurants cater to Vinitaly attendees, offering discounts to those who present their printed exhibition pass. Reserve early for the dining experience of a lifetime. Antico Caffe Dante, the superb restaurant located in Piazza Dante, after famed Italian author Dante Alighieri (*Inferno*, *Divine Comedy*, etc.), pairs rare wines with culinary delicacies that would make connoisseurs cry with satisfaction. The famed restaurant Antica Bottega del Vino, renowned since 1891 for its victuals, boasts one of the most extensive wine lists in Italy. It's not a list so much as a chapter book of varietals over which any wine lover would drool.

No matter your expertise or your palate, Vinitaly has something to offer wine lovers of every caliber. Plan now for the event of a lifetime. For more information on accommodations, an exhibition guide, a list of vendors, and ticket registration for Vinitaly, go to http://vinitaly.com.

HUNGRY FOR OPERA

Hungry for Italian opera? Me too. Conversely, Italian opera makes me hungry. As in, ravenous for a full-course meal, every time. I don't know whether it's something about the brilliant orchestra, or the talented actors, or the musical compositions themselves that evokes my hunger. What I do know, the little snack bar stocked with peanuts, candy bars, and crackers is never enough to sate my appetite.

When I studied Italian opera at the University of Rome, part of my midterm included attending an evening showing of *Don Giovanni* at Teatro dell'Opera di Roma, an iconic nineteenth-century theater. By the time my classmate and now husband, Jamie, and I made it to the end of the first act, a craving for tortellini struck me so hard that not even the lascivious character Don Juan could keep me in my seat until the end. Jamie and I dashed through the cobblestone streets in the dark of night in search of fresh cheese-filled pasta and a hearty Bolognese sauce. We thoroughly enjoyed Mozart's music and the libretto by Lorenzo Da Ponte, but it's the memory of my quest for pasta in high heels that stays with me.

A few years back, hunger pangs struck again at the opera, this time halfway through Giuseppe Verdi's four-part adaptation of Shakespeare's *Macbeth* at the world-renowned La Scala in Milan. In my defense, I made it through two very long acts, amid the red velvet and golden gloriousness of the opera house, seated in the balcony high above the stage. Breathing the air up there apparently builds an appetite. Also, if you love risotto, Milan is the best place to experience this lavish dish of Arborio rice with a touch of saffron, especially when a chef tosses in porcini mushrooms as a random act of kindness. How could I have resisted?

Jamie and I celebrated his father's eightieth birthday with tickets to Giacomo Puccini's *La Boheme* at Boston's Schubert Theatre. Even our children were captivated by the glorious opening aria, until our stomachs growled, echoing loudly in the mezzanine. Jamie and I, with the kids in tow, dashed outside to street level, downed a couple hot Italian sausage and peppers from a street vendor right outside, and made it back before Jamie's parents even noticed we were gone. The final aria of the performance was heartbreaking and beautiful, and poor Jamie suffered heartburn. He was fine by the time we arrived at our North End restaurant for the birthday dinner. A pasta fix, a slice of tiramisu, and a heated discussion over the similarities and differences of *La Boheme*, *Rent* and *Les Misérables* set things right.

There's an Italian opera for every appetite. Some are more palatable than others, depending on length and plotline. Some are romantic, others witty or tragic, and still others deliver a serious social message. Generally, performances are engaging and memorable, and they are many to choose from, depending on whether it's date night, an afternoon with friends, or a semiannual cultural outing with the kids. Some of the most popular Italian operas include Rossini's *The Barber of Seville* and *Othello*; Verdi's *La Traviata*, *Aida*, and *Rigoletto*; and Puccini's *Tosca* and *Turandot*. Be sure to check out tickets to shows in any American city during opera season, or else travel to any Italian city, as performances typically run all year.

I admire the fortitude of most theatergoers who are able to suppress their appetite and thoroughly enjoy a full opera straight to the end. But if you're like me, be prepared to take an unorthodox yet fulfilling pasta run midway through a thrilling performance. The beauty of any opera performance is always best appreciated on a full stomach.

AUTO RACING

One of my favorite sports that I love to watch is championship open-wheel auto racing, because I have so many fond memories of Sunday afternoons as a child spent with my dad enjoying the IndyCar or Formula One races on TV while my mom cooked us the best pot roast ever.

We'd watch the lights go from red to green, signaling the suspenseful start. We'd wonder who would overtake who in the opening laps while the drivers vied for position. We'd count out loud the seconds that elapsed during pit stops. Sometimes I'd close my eyes just to listen to the engines buzz around the track, or to savor the accents of the European announcers. And the exciting climax of the race always promised the wave of a checkered flag and Mom's home cooking. That's why one of my dreams is to attend an IndyCar or Formula One race, where the sights and sounds of one of the world's most exhilarating sports will take place live, right in front of my eyes.

Auto racing has been a mainstay in Italian sports for decades, since racers like Enzo Ferrari (founder of Scuderia Ferrari racing team), Giuseppe "Nino" Farina (winner of the first world championship race and title in 1950), and Alberto Ascari (winner of back-to-back titles in 1952 and 1953) made their marks in history. And who could forget Italian-born Mario Andretti, who won the 1978 Formula One title and four IndyCar championships driving for the United States? The Andretti car-racing lineage also continues with his son, Michael (winner of an IndyCar title), and his grandson, Marco (the first third-generation recipient of the Rookie of the Year Award).

Though my love for auto racing runs deep, I'm a little sheepish to admit that I've never yet attended a race. But I've gotten pretty close. Once I visited the Monaco Formula One Grand Prix street circuit—one day after the big race. Still, I hoofed the hairpin turn in my flip-flops, jogged past the enormous pool, and waved to the yachts on the harbor. Walking the route was like a dream come true, amid the lingering smell of gasoline and burnt tire rubber, where Ayrton Senna had just won the day before.

I long to witness an F1 or IndyCar race in person, where cars take to the course in all their glory, as just one of thousands of spectators who line the streets on a hot weekend with a front-row seat for the festivities. I'd love to catch a glimpse of the sport's big names, like Helio Castroneves, Scott Dixon, Ryan Hunter-Reay, or Marco Andretti.

Last year, I pulled on my racing gloves and my balaclava, and I raced my V-6 Honda CR-V the entire track of the famed Circuit Gilles Villeneuve, in Montreal, Canada, at breakneck speeds topping thirty-five miles per hour, with the wind on my face and bugs in my teeth. Alas, it was the off-season and my only competitors were the seagulls and a couple of black squirrels, but it was a thrill for me.

My love for the sport also imbues the characters in my thriller novels. In *The Race*, my auto-racing covert agent, Devlin Lucchesi, and his HELL Ranger crew save Rome. The racer returns in my novel *Formula*, where Devlin investigates the murder of his colleague at the Monaco Grand Prix. There's just something so exciting and mysterious about the sport that it drives me to write more thrilling stories about these characters every day. Learn more at www.GinaFava.com.

That's why, though I love to watch auto racing on TV, I'm excited for the opportunity to experience the sights and sounds of the race live and in person. Why not join me this year and take a moment to get your blood racing? Plan a dream vacation to a European track like the one in Monza, Italy. Or check out the F1 race held in Texas every November. Or else scan the IndyCar schedule for details and tickets about other American tracks. *Forza!*

SIENA'S PALIO:
TRADITION, COMPETITION, & PRIDE

Imagine that your favorite team is scheduled to compete in the biggest sporting event of the year, smack dab in the center of your hometown. Pack the venue with over fifty thousand spectators, both local and international, all there to see your team participate. Now bring on all the fanfare and hoopla in the days leading up to the main event, including an open-air feast and a ritual blessing of the key player. Now imagine that this monumental sporting event lasts just seventy-five seconds...

For the people of Siena, Italy, this fantasy is a reality. Considered Italy's most famous annual sporting event, Palio is a horse race that combines pageantry, competition, and civic pride. The Tuscan hillside town of Siena fans out from the central shell-shaped Piazza del Campo town square, where the race is run, and extends outward through the maze of cobblestone alleyways, stone houses, shops, and smaller piazze. Siena is divided into seventeen contrade, akin to the boroughs of Manhattan, in which neighborhoods aspire to a passionate regionalism based on centuries-old tradition. Since the Middle Ages, ten of the contrade vie for bragging rights achieved by a victory in a bareback horse race that's one lap around the piazza. The first horse to cross the finish line, with or without the rider, wins.

The race, held twice a year on July 2 and August 16, is preceded by as much pomp and circumstance as the post-race victory parties. Participants and spectators have been brought to their knees over a loss, or a win. Every stage is critical, from the initial presentation of the horses, to the *tratta*, in which the horses and jockeys are matched. It continues with the five preliminary runs, to the final rehearsal dinner, to the blessing of the horse and jockey inside the contrada's parish church, and finally to the race.

I attended my first Palio with my dad when I was ten years old, joining revelers from our contrada, known as Aquila. With my Aquila scarf wrapped securely around my shoulders, I cheered parade flag-bearers marching down the ancient cobblestone streets while my gelato ran down my arm. We watched a trial run that made my head spin. My favorite part was the pre-race dinner. I couldn't believe that with all the eating, the drinking, the singing, and the cheering, they had yet to run the race! Though we missed the main race due to travel, the pre-game festivities were something truly memorable.

Years later, my husband, Jamie, and I made it to the big event. We packed into Piazza del Campo with my cousins in the early morning…and waited. For hours beneath the August sun, the piazza filled with spectators, standing shoulder to shoulder, or peering out from hotel windows overlooking the track. Fans from competing contrade would argue, laugh, make bets, and proudly wave their flags' colors. At dusk, the tension was palpable. The crowds roared as the horses cantered into the piazza. The tradition of centuries past, and the competitive spirit roiling between the contrade, and the anxiety built up over days of preparation all came down to a race lasting just over a minute. In one mad dash around the track, colors blazed past us in a blur. Men, women, and children shouted and chanted the names of their contrada. Cameras flashed. Hoof-beaten dust flew into the humid Sienese twilight. I honestly don't remember who won. (I bet it was Aquila.) But for me, the race was up there with the Super Bowl and the Stanley Cup Final.

Like a good thriller, Palio's suspense builds to a satisfying climax that resonates with fans long after it ends. That's why it played a part in my latest novel, *Formula*. Want to live the thrill? Head to Palio yourself. Plan your visit at www.DiscoverTuscany.com.

SEASONS

FORAGING FOR PRANZO:
THE HUNT FOR WILD EDIBLES

Who knew foraging for something wild to eat could reap such fulfilling rewards? It's the primal adventure of traipsing through the woods, a lush field, or the base of an olive grove and getting your hands and knees dirty in search of sustenance. It's the pleasure of transforming those overlooked gems of nature into delectable fare like omelettes, pasta sauces, salads, soups, or desserts that's so gratifying. Plus, the gathering of family and friends in celebration of the bounty under a canopy of trees on a hillside or in a park often yields lifelong memories. Generations of Italians uphold this tradition of foraging as an adventure, a hobby, or just part of preparing any meal, in Italy and in America. Spring and fall are the perfect times of year to skip the grocery store and head outdoors for some fresh, wild ingredients.

One of my favorite memories as a girl was the time I foraged through the woods on Mount Amiata with my dad's family. Tuscan locals typically pride themselves on sneaking away in the early morning or late afternoon to scavenge alone for the perfect porcini, wild garlic, dandelion, wild radish, chickweed, or stinging nettle. But my dad's aunts, uncles, and cousins often went all together on a weekend, with children and dogs joining in on the hunt. That's what we did that day.

My dad put on old shoes, strapped on a canteen of water and a small satchel for our finds, pocketed his Swiss Army knife for digging and cutting, and ventured out, but only after he'd found the perfect sturdy walking stick. The rest of us joined him, usually many paces behind his brisk pace, because he wanted to be the first one to discover something. After a few hours, we all spilled onto picnic blankets and tables and feasted on what we'd brought from home, too fearful to eat what we'd found until we checked with the experts back in town. The adults dragged out the homemade wine and laughed and told stories, making new memories without even knowing it. Later in the evening, my nana and her sisters cooked the mushrooms and herbs as the filling for ravioli, and dried some of them for use in future recipes.

Growing up in America, my brothers and I were raised on this tradition when my mom and dad took us to explore the woods of Allegany State Park, mostly for wild raspberries on an undiscovered path. Every year, to commemorate our annual adventure, my dad would seek out the largest porcini. He'd carve his kids' names on it, dry it, and later display it on a shelf, far more valuable to us as a memento than as a food source. Also, my grandpa collected the dandelions from his backyard and cooked them down with oil and garlic, a delicious delicacy that we only appreciated years later. The joy continues with my own children, born scavengers, whether in the fields and forests of the United States or back in Italy.

Springtime in Italy means that wild asparagus abounds, as common as blades of grass, and savory with butter and wild garlic. In the fall, Italians keep an eye out for all sorts of mushroom varieties. (In Tuscany, there are rules for hunting them, including size restrictions and the requirement of obtaining a license. See www.regione.toscana.it for details.) For those who want to embark on their own foraging adventures, there are plenty throughout the country. In the Northeast, check out www.wildfoodgirl.com and www.joshfecteau.com for monthly guides from March through November on foraging through the seasons. Take a look at www.emikodavies.com to learn more about the array of weeds, tips for foraging, and recipes for enjoying the bounty. To serve up those traditional, earthy just-found wild flavors in delicious dishes, grab your walking stick and enjoy the hunt!

SKI SEASON

Why not make the most of the coldest, snowiest time of year like I do, by strapping on a pair of skis or a snowboard and hurtling down the nearest mountain? As a native Buffalonian who's grown up on the slopes of Kissing Bridge and Holiday Valley ski resorts, as well as a decades-long resident of New England who's braved subzero temperatures in winter, I figure: if you can't beat 'em, join 'em. Many Italians also hit the slopes, here and in Italy, because it's a great way to transform the winter doldrums into winter fun. Though, whenever I ski with my husband, Jamie, it always reminds me of the time when we first started dating, and he did everything in his power to impress me with his schussing prowess.

While I was studying abroad in Rome during college, my Italian cousins treated me to a holiday in the Dolomites, an Alpine region in Italy that spans across Veneto, Alto-Adige, and Trentino. (I was so spellbound by the magnificent, yet mysterious region, which is dotted by gorges, cliffs, tiny towns, and the bustling city of Verona, that I set the characters of my latest novel, *Formula*, into the wine region there.)

On the trip, my cousins and I traveled about seven hours by car to the small town of Campitello, in the Val di Fassa region of the mountain range, and bunked with friends in their home. The first day, we woke before dawn and hit the slopes until sunset. When we returned to the villa in town, we found Jamie in the main square, with a fever, chills, and a horrible sore throat, shivering alone on a snowbank in a paper-thin parka that he'd borrowed from a Vatican priest. He'd hopped a bus the night before, knowing only the name of the town, and nearly twenty hours later, he'd arrived in Campitello, praying to run into us before nightfall. Ah, young love.

We hauled Jamie inside and plied him with soup, wine, and blankets, and then took his temperature … 104 degrees! A cousin rushed him to the local doctor, acquired antibiotics for his strep throat, and then put him up next door at an inn. After sleeping through the night, and the next day, and the next night, he awoke healthy and joined us, ready to ski. We hotdogged down those slopes for two full days, some of the best skiing ever.

During a more recent visit to Italy, I again visited my family in Abbadia San Salvatore, a small town in the Tuscan hills near Montalcino, where my young cousins and I skied on Mount Amiata, the site of La Croce del Monte Amiata, a beautiful steel cross where hikers climb in summer and that glistens magnificently when covered in snow in winter. Though the slopes there were considerably shorter and less steep than those in the Dolomites, the experience of skiing with family near my father's hometown was truly memorable.

Since then, my Italian relatives have come to love and appreciate Jamie, though they've never skied with him again, too much trouble. But he and I continue to escape to the mountains near Boston for romantic ski dates. Many resorts in New England that feature skiing, snowboarding, and tubing, all provide a taste of the sport that rivals the action in the Dolomites. We have our eyes on Colorado and Utah in the future. I love spending vacation with family, friends, or my sweetheart on the slopes in winter. What better way to stay warm than cuddling on the chairlift or sipping cocoa by the fire in the lodge?

MERCATO TREASURES

Just like fresh air revitalizes the soul, open-air markets stimulate the senses. Rain or shine, tented tables regularly bring neighbors, tourists, and communities together from spring to fall, providing a taste of Earth's bounty and a vast assortment of handmade collectibles and vintage wares. Grab your family and meet your friends at an open-air market, because a visit there is not always about what objects you procure but rather the experience you'll savor.

Crates overflowing with just-ripened fruits and vegetables, iced pallets of succulent seafood pulled from the water earlier that morning, and bunches of aromatic flowers at the peak of color abound in a random assortment of tables along the street or grass. Artisans and collectors mingle too, to celebrate handmade works like tapestries, pottery, jewelry, or paintings that are all unique among any other. Vendors also pile tables high with vintage items like leather goods, music, small appliances, shoes, ravioli cutters, or any odd thing, sometimes authentic and sometimes not. Here, one person's odds and ends are another person's treasure.

.   In Italy, one doesn't have to venture far to find a local open-air market, but there are some in bigger cities that are worth noting for their size, variety, and ambience, such as the Campo de' Fiori, a fish and vegetable market in Rome dating back to 1869. Open from 7 a.m. to 1 p.m., Monday through Saturday, the cobblestone piazza is filled with vendors even before the sun comes up. An Ape Piaggio (a compact three-wheeled truck) sits beside nearly every tent, piled high with crates of fresh food. Before it opens, restaurant buyers examine the selections for the highest-quality ingredients, and by noon, tourists stare in awe at the shouting matches as the elderly locals haggle with vendors in preparation for their pranzo meal.

The Porta Portese market in Trastevere, Rome, open Sundays, showcases table after table of anything imaginable, including terra cotta, oil lamps, and toothbrushes. In college, I bought a cheap bootleg copy there of Sting's *The Dream of the Blue Turtles* cassette tape (yes, cassette tape!) and when I got it home, I was disappointed to learn that the B side of the "hot" tape featured an entirely different band, named Zucchero. Little did I realize that this was one of Italy's hottest bands, and that months later I would watch both Sting and Zucchero perform at Rome's Stadio Olimpico arena together. The value of some bazaar treasures truly surpasses dollars and cents.

A few years ago, my parents accompanied me and my family to Venice, where we hit the famed Rialto Market early enough that the garbage boats were still hauling away rubbish left by the overnight revelers. At the fish market, vendors slapped enormous large-fin saltwater monsters onto their tables of chopped ice, while my dad giggled like a kid in a candy store. My children's eyes were almost as big as those of the enormous multicolored fish they ogled. After a couple hours, I spied my mom cuddling with my youngest, Mario, sharing a lovely moment beside a canal. As their legs dangled over the Adriatic inlet, red juice dripped down their fingers, their only market takeaway having been a quart of the juiciest strawberries sold at the fruit stand beneath the Rialto Bridge. Some treasures are meant to be consumed without delay, and with total abandon.

The town of Camucia, near Cortona in Tuscany, opens its market on Thursdays, cordoning off about ten city blocks, where a delectable pulled-pork sandwich is just as easy to find among its multitude of merchants as a new suitcase. And in Palermo, Sicily, one can peruse seaside tables of sea urchins and other such delicacies that are just as plentiful as oranges. The art of seeking out-of-the-way treasures may be just as decadent as the object itself.

But in the States, one need not venture far for a great open-air market. There's probably one within driving distance, and it's so worth the time and gasoline. Growing up in Buffalo, my dad used to drive my grandpa to the Clinton Market whenever it was time to buy the perfect crops for their new gardens. Now, my brothers take my dad whenever they're ready to plant theirs. Easter week, my family would head to the also-famous Broadway Market for freshly packed sausage, homemade bread, and the best fire-breathing horseradish around. We still go there, but now we also frequent the food trucks and vendors at Larkin Square and Canalside, among many others. The buddy-system always makes for a memorable market experience.

Haymarket, Boston's historic market near Faneuil Hall since 1830, is renowned for its produce and fish, at bargain prices. Haggling here is a must-see tourist attraction in the city. Head over to Copley Place Farmers Market in the Back Bay for homemade apple pies, jams, and spreads, or armfuls of bright yellow sunflowers. Lose yourself for hours at the SoWa Market ("South of Washington Street") for an eclectic mix of handmade items, like jewelry, crafts, pottery, shoes, and baked goods, as well as antiques and fresh produce. Local open markets abound in every major city and in many small towns across America. If you're like me, an Italian who loves to buy fresh and buy local, you'll want to be sure to experience any one of these glorious markets as the season warms and the treasures are ripe for the picking. Bring your family and friends, and revel in the spirit of *abbondanza*!

FOR THE LOVE OF FIGS

"How many figs do *you* have on your tree?" This is all I hear during harvest season in my family. Over the past few years, my husband, my dad, and my two younger brothers, Tony and Joey, have each acquired fig trees for their yards. Since the first year of cultivating them, these men have relentlessly competed over quantity of fruit. My mom and I have never complained, because among their trees, the quality of the fruit never wavers—plump, ripe, hearty delicious figs make it to the table every year.

Figs are among the oldest cultivated crops, grown by the ancient Egyptians, Romans, and Greeks. In Italy, it's a proud landowner who grows fig trees, and that's why some of the Italian men in my life tend to theirs with such care and pride. Figs are grown on deciduous trees that typically reach ten to twenty feet tall and may bear anywhere from dozens to hundreds of walnut-sized fleshy fruit per year.

There are a number of varieties, each adapted to growing regions. Typically, figs are semitropical trees that do well in zones with longer, warmer seasons. However, for those living in the Northeast growing zone, growing fig trees is still possible. It just requires a bit more nurturing. Varieties common to the Northeast are: Brown Turkey, Celeste, Dark Portuguese, LSU Gold, Brooklyn White, and Purple Genca. One can buy young trees locally at farmer's markets or online from reputable growers who will ship them to your door.

Jamie, Tony, Joey, and my dad all keep their figs trees in large base pots, atop wheeled platforms. The trees thrive in the brightest spot in their yards all summer, with regular watering and fertilization. Fruit is usually harvested anywhere between the end of August and the beginning of October for maximum texture and rich, juicy flavor.

At the first sign of temperatures dipping below fifty degrees, they roll the trees into their garages, where they remain dormant through the winter. Further care depends on the type and hardiness of the tree and the harshness of the temperatures. My dad insists on wrapping his in burlap, though Jamie does not. Other growers have suggested a newspaper and burlap wrap for added warmth, and even a bucket on top of that layer. Still others have said that they tip the plant on its side and drape an old rug over the branches.

Once spring arrives, do not rush the plant back into the yard. Radical temperature variations will shock the tree (the leaves will drop and the crop will become stunted) or even damage the tree irreparably. It's better to remove the layers within the shelter of a shed or garage and then move it outdoors when the warm weather stabilizes. Of course, growing fig trees inside a greenhouse all year long will guarantee its resistance to the elements.

There's nothing quite like kicking back during the summer and enjoying the beauty and the bounty that fig trees provide. For me, the true enjoyment comes during harvest season. Pluck one right from the tree, sink your teeth into a rosy, plump fruit, and let the juice run down your chin. Gather a few, cut them in half, and sprinkle them with powdered sugar for a fresh, healthy dessert. Tantalize your dinner guests with an appetizer that takes minutes to prepare: cut a bunch of figs in half, top with parmesan shavings, drizzle with balsamic vinegar, and pop them in the broiler for three minutes. Finally, don't forget the fresh fig cookies that you can make at Christmastime! Recipes abound, and so do the memories, when families share in the joy of homegrown figs.

HOLY MACKEREL:
'TWAS THE NIGHT BEFORE CHRISTMAS

Imagine stepping out of the blustery, snowy, icy, dark December cold and into a warm, brightly lit, steam-windowed, pots-bubbling-over kitchen where the white-haired apron-clad chefs cease their chopping, broiling, and stirring just for a moment to enfold you in their tender, welcoming arms and then order you and your entire family to sit down and eat while they proudly serve up course after course of the most aromatic, succulent, and mouthwatering dishes. Ah, the delectable wonder of Christmas Eve.

When I was growing up, my family embraced the Christmas Eve tradition of the Feast of the Seven Fishes. Roman Catholics observe the holy day known by Italians as *La Vigilia di Natale*, the vigil of the birth of the baby Jesus, by abstaining from meat, and my grandparents would simmer, sauté, and stew as many types of fish as they could muster into a dinner that began right after four-o'clock mass and lasted until our full bellies kept us from hoisting another platter around the table.

When the food was ready, Nana dabbed the perspiration from her nose and combed her lustrous white hair in the mirror. Grandpa took his seat at the head of the table, and our family bowed heads for a prayer. While Nana would recite the Profession of Faith in her native tongue, my dad would smack my brothers' hands that surreptitiously sought nibbles of every dish before she finished. Grandpa would then pour his homemade red wine into tumblers that our noses could barely fit into, and Nana would top off the glasses with ginger ale for the children. (Yes, I'm convinced my grandmother invented the "spritz.") Finally, plates were passed and chaos reigned. "*Mangia*, baby, and shut up," my grandpa would tell his young grandchildren with a smile on his face, and we would feast.

While the tradition calls for seven fish, my nana firmly believed that there was never enough food on the table and always added a few more dishes to the menu. Our seven fish, fresh from the market, typically included:

1. Fried calamari (squid);
2. Octopus, whose tentacles and suckers were breaded and fried to perfection;
3. Eel stew, cooked in tomato broth that still couldn't hide the thick black eel;
4. Baccalà, a dry, salted cod that Grandpa would soak for an entire day before baking, stewing, or sautéing (just watch out for the bones!);
5. Fresh sardines;
6. Fresh mackerel (with its eyes staring up at you right from the oven); and
7. Fresh, cooked cold shrimp.

The savory extras thrown in for good measure might include:

- Pasta with anchovies;
- Cauliflower and bread salad with canned sardines, olive oil, and vinegar;
- A plate of fried artichokes; or
- A fresh, thick bulb of *fenocchio* (anise) with a dish of olive oil and salt and pepper for dipping.

Where's the dessert? We'd put off the decadent treats until Christmas Day, when my mom would serve her delicious homemade pies and cookies. Instead, we washed down our vigil feast with a little *digestivo* and some assorted nuts and oranges. Nana and Grandpa could finally sit back and revel in the happy, fulfilled looks on their children's sated faces and sip a bit of Strega liqueur or some coffee with a bit of anisette. Nana would remove her apron, smile, and let out a contented sigh while she sipped her steaming espresso to the sound of cracking walnuts, hazelnuts, and almonds. Grandpa would unseal and pass a mason jar of homemade peaches that he'd packed in thick syrup the past summer. My dad would impress the little ones by twisting an orange peel into the candle flame thereby creating a mini-flamethrower, and then shock them with a little squirt of the citrus oil in the eye to keep them on their toes before Santa arrived.

Looking back, I'm not sure what I appreciate most about the annual feast. It might have been the dining room table set with glimmering china and glassware, the steaming plates of abundant food, and the ravenous eyes twinkling amid the high, tapered candles. Maybe it was the laughter, and the sharing of exotic delicacies with a family that seemed to outgrow the table every year. Or else it was the drowsy, drunk-with-food-and-wine faces, slumped on elbows atop the delicate Burano lace tablecloth strewn with nutshells and orange peels. I'm sure it's the perfect combination of all of it. *Buon Natale, tutti.*

RECIPES

Dad's Tapenade

My dad typically makes this spicy appetizer to serve at Christmastime, but it's a mouthwatering dip or spread for any occasion during the year. My dad makes extra and gives jars of it to his lucky kids.

*Jamie's wine pairing: Pinotage

Ingredients:

- **1 large container mixed olives (black and green, pitted, w/olive oil, red pepper flakes, garlic)**
- **5+ cloves of garlic**
- **1–2 heaping Tbsp. capers**
- **A pinch of red pepper flakes and oregano to taste**
- **1–2 pepperoncino or jalapeno peppers as desired**
- **Olive oil**

Directions:

1. **Add ingredients to food processor and pulse until coarsely chopped.**
2. **Add olive oil to desired consistency.**
3. **Serve at room temperature on toasted baguette crostini.**

Grandpa's Broccoli Rabe

Grandpa would take hours to make this, because he was so meticulous about chopping the greens just right. But it's actually quick and easy to make. It works well as a side dish, and Grandpa used to pile some onto slices of bread with grated Romano cheese for a sandwich. You can freeze leftovers into single-serving size.

*Jamie's wine pairing: Viognier

Ingredients:

- **3 stalks/bunches of fresh broccoli rabe (cut off thick stems, chop small)**
- **4–5 cloves sliced garlic per bunch**
- **Olive oil**
- **1/2 in. fresh red pepper or 1/2 tsp. red pepper flakes**

Directions:

1. **Cover bottom of pan with olive oil.**
2. **Sauté garlic and add broccoli rabe and red pepper**
3. **Add 3/4–1 c. water per bunch (do not cover with water, just let steam)**
4. **Salt and pepper to taste.**
5. **Cover pot and cook to al dente.**

Mom's Green Bean/Gina's Fava Bean Salad

Mom always makes this refreshing salad for outdoor picnics and barbecues, but its heartiness makes it a great side dish for any meal. Her recipe features fresh green beans from the garden or market.

I improvised, because Gina Fava is partial to fava beans.

*Jamie's wine pairing: Collio Pino Grigio

Ingredients:

- **4 c. shucked fresh fava beans (or whole green beans)**
- **3 c. potatoes, chopped**
- **2-3 medium fresh tomatoes, chopped**
- **1 cucumber, diced**
- **1 small red onion, sliced or chopped**
- **2 cloves, minced**
- **Olive oil and vinegar**
- **Basil, oregano, salt, and pepper to taste**

Directions:

1. **Boil beans and potatoes until tender.**
2. **Mix all ingredients.**
3. **Toss with oil and vinegar, and season.**
4. **Cover and refrigerate for at least three hours.**

Gina's Breaded Cauliflower

This recipe is great as a vegetable side dish. It's also a quick and easy vegetarian appetizer for book club gatherings.

* Jamie's wine pairing: Unoaked Chardonnay

Ingredients:

- **1 head of fresh cauliflower**
- **1-2 eggs, beaten**
- **Flour**
- **1 c. bread crumbs**
- **Olive oil**
- **Red pepper flakes, salt and pepper, parmesan cheese to taste**

Directions:

1. **Break apart head of cauliflower into bite-size florets. Parboil them in salted water until al dente.**
2. **Pat dry. Dip in egg, then flour, then egg, then bread crumbs.**
3. **Cover bottom of pan with olive oil. Sauté until golden brown; OR**
4. **Bake at 350 degrees for twenty-five minutes for a healthy choice.**
5. **Season and sprinkle with parmesan cheese.**

Gina's Artichoke Dip

This dip is rich, creamy, and decadent. It's another great appetizer for a book club get-together, but it goes fast!

*Jamie's wine pairing: Oregon Pinot Noir

Ingredients:

- **2 cans artichoke hearts**
- **2-3 c. shredded mozzarella cheese**
- **1 cup mayonnaise**
- **3/4 c. parmesan cheese**
- **3 cloves garlic, chopped fine**
- **Paprika to taste**

Directions:

1. **Drain artichokes well, chop fine.**
2. **Mix all ingredients in small casserole dish.**
3. **Sprinkle with paprika.**
4. **Bake at 325 degrees for 20-25 minutes, until golden brown.**
5. **Serve with pita chips or toasted baguette crostini. You can serve it as a spread atop Gina's Bruschetta (See recipe below.)**

Gina's Bruschetta

Bruschetta is a great snack or appetizer because you can change up the toppings every time you serve it. Italians love to offer it as a snack with an Aperol Spritz (See Jamie's recipe.) It's also another great appetizer for a book club party. (Can you tell how much I love book clubs?) This recipe is a basic one. Feel free to change the type of cheese, or the toppings, or the sauce, or even the bread. Have fun!

*Jamie's wine pairing: Valdobbiadene Prosecco

Ingredients:

- **1 baguette loaf, sliced at an angle for maximum surface area**
- **2-3 c. shredded mozzarella cheese**
- **1 c. pesto sauce**
- **1 c. tomatoes, diced**
- **3/4 c. parmesan cheese**
- **3 cloves garlic, chopped fine**

Directions:

1. **Arrange the baguette crostini on a baking tray. Broil until lightly toasted.**
2. **Remove from oven. Spread sauce. Sprinkle toppings and cheese.**
3. **Broil just until cheese is melted and golden brown.**

Mom's Pasta e Fagioli

This is comfort food at its finest. Growing up, I used to sit in the kitchen and do homework while Mom prepared dinner. I never learned to cook a thing until years later when I had to, but our time for sharing conversation was more nurturing than anything she ever cooked. Her soup is good, too.

*Jamie's wine pairing: Montepulciano d'Abruzzo

Ingredients:

- **2 Tbsp. olive oil**
- **2 large cloves garlic, chopped**
- **One 15-oz. can cannellini beans**
- **4 medium potatoes, diced**
- **2 Tbsp. canned tomato paste**
- **1-2 c. water, to desired consistency of soup or stew**
- **Red pepper flakes to taste**
- **Salt and pepper to taste**
- **2 tsp. apple cider vinegar**
- **1-2 c. ditalini, cooked al dente**
- **Grated Parmigiano or Romano cheese, for the table**

Directions:

1. Heat a pot over medium high heat, and add oil and potatoes. Soften, but do not brown.

2. Add garlic and red pepper flakes. Cook but do not brown.

3. Add tomato paste and beans. Crush a few beans to thicken.

4. Add water until about halfway up the mixture. Salt and pepper.

5. Cover and simmer on medium until potatoes are soft, about an hour. Add more water as desired.

6. Add apple cider vinegar for extra zing, and cook for 5 or 10 minutes.

7. Let stand 5 minutes. Add hot, cooked ditalini and serve. Top with grated cheese.

Gina's Chicken with Olives

This recipe is derived from one that Jamie's Nana Josie used to make, with a few spicy adjustments. It's the dish that my dad requests whenever he visits. There are rarely leftovers.

*Jamie's wine pairing: Roero Arneis

Ingredients:

- **1 lb. chicken thighs**
- **1 lb. chicken drumsticks**
- **2–3 chicken breasts**
- **2–3 cloves garlic (whole)**
- **1 large yellow onion, sliced**
- **1/2 lb. container of fresh, pitted Kalamata olives**
- **1/2–3/4 c. balsamic vinegar**
- **1/4 c. dry white wine**
- **1 tsp. sugar to reduce acidity**
- **1 dry bay leaf**
- **2 dashes parsley**
- **2 dashes oregano**
- **2 dashes basil**
- **2 dashes red pepper flakes**
- **Salt and pepper to taste**
- **Olive oil**
- **Water**

Directions:

1. Cover the bottom of a large skillet in olive oil. Brown the chicken on medium heat.

2. Add the garlic and onions.

3. Add the wine and let simmer 5 minutes.

4. Add the vinegar and olives.

5. Sprinkle in the sugar and spices.

6. Let simmer on low for an hour, adding water as needed.

7. Remove garlic cloves. Let stand for 5 minutes. Serve with fresh bread. Yields 4–6 servings.

Nana's Jam Tart (Costata di Marmellata)

Nana and Grandpa were known for making the best main dishes, but never dessert. This one is a delicious exception. And it's extra special because Nana would make it for our annual Easter breakfast feast. *Buona Pasqua!*

*Jamie's wine pairing: Vin Santo

Ingredients:

- **1 12 oz. jar of jam (any flavor)**
- **1 egg (beaten)**
- **Sweet Pie Pastry:**
  - **2 c. flour**
  - **2/3 c. butter**
  - **1 egg**
  - **2 Tbsp. sugar**
  - **3–4 Tbsp. chilled white wine**
    - **Blend butter and flour. Add egg, sugar and wine. Work into ball. Wrap in waxed paper and refrigerate for 1 hour.**

Directions:

1. Grease a pie plate or cake tin.
2. Set aside 1/3 of the dough for lattice decoration.
3. Roll out remainder of dough to a 12 in. circle.
4. Place in pan, and prick bottom with fork.
5. Spread jam in pastry. Roll out reserved dough to 1/8 in. thickness.
6. Cut into 3/4 in. strips with a ravioli cutter or serrated knife.
7. Create lattice across top of jam.
8. Brush dough with beaten egg.
9. Bake at 375 degrees 30–40 minutes or until golden brown.
10. Let stand 30 minutes before removing from pan. Serves 10 slices.

My Family's Easter (or Anytime) Lamb

This lamb recipe is a hearty, flavorful dish that would be perfect as a main meal during the winter months. But for our family, it's a springtime entrée for our traditional Easter breakfast, no not brunch, rather breakfast, right after mass and before Mom and Dad's wild Easter egg hunt.

*Jamie's wine pairing: Côte du Rhone

Ingredients:

- **2 lb. fresh bone-in lamb, cut into thin pieces with bone by butcher**
- **1/4 c. medium onion, diced**
- **1 clove garlic, minced**
- **1/2 c. dry white wine**
- **1/4 c. white vinegar**
- **1-2 bay leaves and sage leaves**
- **Salt, pepper, rosemary, and red pepper flakes to taste**

Directions:

1. **Brown lamb in large skillet with olive oil.**
2. **Sauté with garlic and onion until they're translucent.**

3. Add all leaves and seasoning. Cover and simmer for 20 minutes.

4. Add white wine. Cook covered 10 minutes, or until lamb is tender.

5. Add vinegar and cook uncovered 5 more minutes.

6. Serve with warm, toasted bread for sopping up the juicy gravy.

Jamie's Pasta

Jamie and I love "Pasta Sunday" at our house. There's nothing like getting your hands dirty, mixing the eggs and flour, and taking turns kneading until our arms are sore. The dogs always end up covered in flour, and our kids tell the best stories while music plays loudly in the background. It's time-consuming hard work. But the meal, and the time spent with family, are so worth it.

*Jamie's wine pairing: Aglianico (from his ancestral region of Campania)

Ingredients:

- **3 c. flour**
- **3 eggs**
- **3 Tbsp. lukewarm water**
- **1/2 tsp. salt**

Directions:

1. **Mix ingredients and knead. Knead.**
2. **Wrap in plastic wrap and refrigerate for 1–2 hours.**
3. **Roll through a pasta machine. The strips are perfect for lasagna or ravioli. Or cut into tagliatelle or spaghetti noodles.**

4. For an extra special treat, go the distance and
   prepare the noodles according to the time-tested
   regional favorite pasta of Tuscany –
   pici! Simply roll each noodle between your fingers
   until thick and long. Serve with your favorite
   sauce.

Nana and Grandpa's Ravioli

Nana and Grandpa created my family's original Pasta Sunday. They'd begin early morning rolling out the pasta to surprise us by noontime with a different dish for every Sunday dinner. One of our favorites is ravioli. The filling is Nana's secret recipe, and the use of the shot glass is Grandpa's claim to fame. It's an arduous process that produces a different texture and consistency every time. It always tastes amazing, and it's an incredibly worthwhile effort, I promise. Jamie would tell you to top it with my homemade Tuscan sauce, but alas, I've been sworn to secrecy. My advice: serve it with a hearty, red meat sauce. This recipe makes about 100 pieces, serving eight people about a dozen pieces each.

*Jamie's wine pairing: Rosso di Montalcino or Nebbiolo

Ingredients:

- **2 lb. ricotta cheese**
- **1 egg**
- **1/2 c. grated romano cheese**
- **10-oz. bag spinach (stems off, cooked down and drained)**
- **1/8 tsp. cinnamon**
- **1/2 tsp. salt**
- **1/8 tsp. pepper**
- **Rolled Pasta (see Jamie's Pasta Recipe)**

Directions:

1. Roll out long 2x4 strips of pasta onto a floured surface.

2. Mix above ingredients.

3. Drop teaspoon dollops of mixture onto pasta strips, an inch apart.

4. Fold over the pasta to envelope the mixture. Press the edges of the pasta with your fingers to seal in the mixture.

5. Dome a shot glass over each dollop, press and seal without breaking the pasta.

6. With a ravioli cutter or knife, cut each ravioli square, leaving about a quarter to a half inch on either side of the dollop.

7. Gingerly add each piece of ravioli to salted, boiling water. Cook about 8-10 minutes, until the pasta is al dente.

Jamie's Aperol Spritz

I'm so lucky to be married to a mixologist/wine expert. Whenever I need a bottle of wine for a particular dish, Jamie pairs the perfect one. And my favorite go-to with appetizers or dessert is Prosecco. The last few times we visited Italy, we noticed the growing popularity of outdoor bars along the main street serving up nibbles and Aperol Spritzes during *la passeggiata*. Back home, we enjoy mixing the refreshing beverage during the spring and summer months or for a party. An Aperol Spritz is light, easy to make, and fun to share for any time of day and any occasion.

Ingredients for a glass (Collins or wine glass):

- **4 ½ oz. Prosecco**
- **2 ½ oz. Aperol**
- **1 oz. chilled seltzer**
- **1 lime or orange, for garnish**
- **Ice**

Ingredients for a pitcher:

- **One 750-mL bottle Prosecco**
- **One 750-mL bottle Aperol**
- **3/4 liter chilled seltzer**
- **1 lime or orange, for garnish**
- **Ice**

Directions: Mix and garnish over ice. Enjoy!

ACKNOWLEDGMENTS

To my readers, thank you for wanting to learn more about my perspective on Italian heritage. There's so much to gain from the vibrant Italian culture, and so much to value about our own particular ways of honoring it. I've already begun collecting more stories and recipes, and I'm hard at work on my next novel. In the meantime…

- Feel free to spread the word about all of my books;
- Write a positive review and share it everywhere;
- Sign up for my "Fava Nuts" newsletter at https://ginafava.com/newsletter for information on new releases, promotions, and special events;
- Follow Gina Fava on Facebook, Twitter, Goodreads, & Instagram;
- Go to www.GinaFava.com to learn more about my books and where to buy them.
- Contact Gina Fava about speaking engagements. I'm always happy to speak with organizations and book clubs, locally or via Skype.

To those that've humbled me in the past with requests to speak with your groups, thank you so much. It's always an honor for me. Special thanks to the editors of *Bostoniano* magazine for publishing many of the original articles. Thank you to Eliza Dee, who edited this book, and Cheryl Perez, who formatted it, with such care and professionalism. Shout out to my local book club friends—for your clever viewpoints and warm hearts, and for vouching for Dad's tapenade.

To Mom, who has taught me how to love with my whole heart. You've taught me right from wrong, encouraged me to be anything I wanted to be, and always put everyone's needs before your own. I love you, a bushel and a peck. To Dad, who successfully braved a new world so that his own family would have a future. You've generously raised your children to exceed your own achievements, and guided us to raise our children to exceed ours. And you cry like a baby when we do. My love for you knows no bounds.

To Nana and Grandpa, who struggled so that their children wouldn't have to. From your kitchen table, your life lessons were served lovingly and in abundance. Your gentle, worn hands crafted keepsakes of style and warmth with yarn, leather, and thread; and nourishment in jars, kettles, and barrels, ensuring generations would remember. To my brothers and sisters, who keep me young. To my nieces and nephews, who are brilliant and magical. Nana and Grandpa must love watching our beautiful children play together.

To Jamie, my soul mate, you're the one who cherishes our heritage more than any of us. This Italian roller coaster is the best in the world. I love you, always and forever. To Sabrina and Mario, you are my joy. I love you with all my heart. Go forth and create your own sauces, ones that will make you truly happy.

To all my relatives, here and across the ocean, who know these stories to be true, and who helped make them possible. *Grazie mille.*

Made in the USA
Columbia, SC
01 November 2018